WHAT LIES BETWEEN US

FOSTERING FIRST STEPS
TOWARD RACIAL HEALING

DR. LUCRETIA CARTER BERRY

WHAT
LIES
BETWEEN
US

ISBN-10: 1544106866
ISBN-13: 978-1544106861

Cover Design: Phil Deppen/Cranial
Interior Design: Betts Keating Design

to Sinclair, London, and Quinn
whose futures inspire this work

Note: To successfully complete this journal, you will need access to the internet and to the documentary, *Race-The Power of an Illusion*. Resource links and access information are shared at Brownicity.com.

CONTENTS

ACKNOWLEDGMENTS

What LIES Between Us is truly a community effort. I am honored to express gratitude

to my husband and partner in love, Nathan and our three little girls (aka The Berry Patch) whose futures inspire this work.

to Jill C. Stallings and her family for all your showing up, praying, babysitting, hand holding, cheerleading, networking, and co-laboring.

to Micaila-Ayorinde Milburn-Thomas, our artist-in-residence for using the arts to help us envision and embody these 'living' lessons.

to Penny Noyes for all your catalyzing wisdom and guidance.

to all the Brownicity friends for having beautiful hearts, for inundating us with lots of questions—which helped shape *What LIES Between Us*—for being our test pilots, for trusting us with your parishioners, for praying, promoting, hosting, attending, volunteering, serving, supporting and encouraging: Pastor Naeem & Ashley Fazal (Mosaic Church, Charlotte), Mike and Debi Adam, Shannon Phelps, Theresa Zeigler, Amy Ray, Tiffany Trudewind, Laura Marti, Lauren Pyles, Patnodes/Hands Missional Community, Phil and Christina Deppen, Kim Honeycutt (icuTalks), Ann Fields, Amanda Goodman, Lisa Stephens, Lisa Madden, Khristian Gutierrez, Pastor Todd Marlin (Independence Hill Baptist Church, Charlotte), Pastors Dan and Anne Berry (Cornerstone Family Church, Des Moines), John Lafferty, and Shannon Bieger.

And a very special 'Thank You' to Pastor Toran C. Smith and family (Body of Christ Church, Ames, IA) for your obedience and courage to launch this in our hearts back in 1997. Haven't we come a long way?

FOREWORD

I'm so proud of my friend Dr. Lucretia Berry. In a world that seems to seek comfortable conversations and surface solutions, Lucretia has dared to go deep to destroy race ideology. Brownicity was born for this reason and I have been privileged to be a part of it from its inception.

Lucretia believes that "the average person is unaware of the damage and deterioration of our society caused by living the 'race' lie." It is this conviction that has led her to create curriculum and conversations to equip people to approach race issues.

We have all seen systemic racism and prejudice at work, but few of us understand the layers or complexity of it in our society. ***What Lies Between Us*** transcends the 'colorblind' point of view that has blinded us to truly see racism. This curriculum gives us eyes to see the framework and the language to address and dismantle racism.

As an immigrant from Kuwait coming to the States in the early 1990's, I had no idea what life would be like. In the time I have lived here, I have never been so hopeful that we as a nation are on the verge of a breakthrough in race issues. But it will take people who are courageous and committed– men, women and children who will create the new normal. I believe Lucretia's passion and voice is one of those daring voices that will bring forth a new dialogue in our country.

Naeem Fazal

Lead Pastor of Mosaic Church, Charlotte
Author of *Ex-Muslim: How One Daring Prayer to Jesus Changed a Life Forever*

❶
WHY?

*Successful transformations reframe the problem
that makes the solution possible.
They erase existing boundaries and start from scratch.*
— Malcolm Gladwell

We are awakening to our collective creative power to heal and change the world. The world will shift quickly when we walk as the light-bearers we were created to be. This requires us to lead the way in dark areas where naturally no one likes to venture. Race/ism is one such area. We've been taught that if we don't talk about race and say we don't see color, racism will go away. Instead this "colorblind" approach has left us void of language and power to confront the darkness of racism as it has continued to divide and conquer us—even in our sacred spaces, like the church. Race/ism is a recent invention that has come to inform how we think about virtually every aspect of our society and culture—and yet we struggle to talk about or even define it. We, the church, are part of the solution for racial healing. We are the light that drives out the darkness. However, as we seek to transform the world, we must first allow ourselves to be transformed. The Apostle Paul told the Romans,

> *Do not allow this world to mold you in its own image. Instead, be transformed from the inside out by renewing your mind. As a result, you will be able to discern what God wills and whatever God finds good, pleasing, and complete.* Romans 12:2 (VOICE)

Likewise, we need to be aware of how we have adopted an ideology that seems to have a stronger influence in and over our lives than our faith. To be a part of the solution for racial healing, we need to understand race/ism and how it has controlled our lives and thoughts—most often without us even recognizing it.

YES, you most likely are a good person and

NO, you don't consider yourself racist.

BUT we ALL have been affected by the race fallacy and its very real legacy, racism. And we all need to understand how deeply we've been affected before we can be a part of the healing and restoration process. We need to clearly see and deconstruct the LIES!

You are here, holding **What LIES Between Us** because you want to be a part of the healing process—you want to be a part of restoration, a part of the solution to the problems created by race/ism. And perhaps your question is *"What do I do?"* The race topic and conversation can be treacherous waters to navigate. So, we have designed this guide, journal, and experience to help equip, empower and inspire you on your journey to becoming a viable part of healing for yourself and others.

WHY DO I NEED A GUIDE?

Chances are, unless you elected to take a course offering a comprehensive study on race, or you attended a skillfully facilitated workshop on race, you have very little experience talking about race in a manner that is healing and life-giving. Chances are most of your race education or lack thereof stems from at least one of these four pretenses:

1. **The "Color Blind" Approach.** Often times and with the best intentions, people will default to this approach believing that we will end racism by pretending not to notice skin color or talk about race/ism. "I don't see color," or "I am colorblind" is often used to assert and assure "I am not racist."

2. **Selectively Skewed History.** Although the United States of America has always had the privilege of being a multi-ethnic nation, the traditional USA history education exclusively centers on European and western conquests, colonization, and contributions.

3. **Human Interest Stories.** Racially incited personal experiences and catastrophic events headlining the news are often shared with no racial historical context.

4. **Political Platforms.** Political platforms are intrinsically divisive, and unfortunately have shaped popular discourse around race/ism. So unknowingly, when many people think they are addressing race/ism, they are actually arguing and projecting a political platform.

None of these pretenses offers the substance needed to have a constructive conversation on race. That's why we refer to them as the *'four false starts!'* We have found that when someone enters the conversation from any of these four starting points, they rarely go in a direction of healing and change. So, we have chosen to highlight and guide you through great content that will help give you a solid foundation upon which to build. Links to the resources we reference and to other great resources can be found on our website, **Brownicity.com**.

WHY DO I NEED A JOURNAL?

Race ideology and our faith are at odds. Answering reflective questions will help awaken us to our subconscious thoughts about race. Because we are unaware of this non-conscious association, much of our thinking and actions stem from unchallenged racial messages we've received all our lives from numerous socializing agents. For example, perhaps you have never had a negative personal encounter with someone of a different ethnicity, but in their presence, you brace yourself anticipating a negative experience. Without even thinking, you are acting out of fear. You are acting against love!

The journal approach is inspired by Dr. Caroline Leaf's program and model for overcoming toxic thinking (*Who Switched Off My Brain? Controlling Toxic Thoughts and Emotions*, 2007). Socialized and conditioned by a hyper-racialized society, we all have unconscious beliefs that we do not choose to have. And many times, our unconscious race-associated beliefs fuel our thinking and actions.

But as Dr. Leaf reminds us, we can change our brains. We can uproot the toxic beliefs that have been planted deep into our psyches by race ideology and racial conditioning. We can renew our minds! As the Apostle Paul alluded in Romans 12:2, we can be transformed and transform our communities.

Answering the journal's reflective questions will help encourage introspection—an examination of our own mental and emotional processes—as we challenge our thinking and actions and renew our minds. The questions are divided into three parts—

1. Reflect

2. Rethink

3. Reach

REFLECT

These questions will help us think about how and where we've gained information about race. Answering these questions will help us become self-aware of our biases. We have all been influenced by social/cultural norms and media, and thus have implicit biases not of our choosing. But we can bring awareness to these unconscious associations and replace them with true information.

A portion of reflective thinking is dedicated to **Reflective Journaling**. In this section, writing out your thoughts will help draw the unconscious into the conscious and allows you to bring clarity to what you've been thinking. Here, we look at our thoughts on paper, and see the areas that need attention. Journaling helps you personally process thoughts and feelings.

RETHINK

These prompts subject our thoughts to our faith. We can break free from the chains of toxic events in our past or stories we have believed. We can uncover our beliefs and actions that create internal conflict with God's words and promises. We can renew our minds. We can align with the truth. We can rewire.

REACH

This section helps us think about how we will reach beyond where we are now. We can change and transform ourselves and the world. We can let God's word come alive in us. We can forgive, pray and do whatever it takes.

WHY THIS PROCESS?

It takes time to unravel and disconnect ourselves from a centuries-old, widely accepted, catastrophic lie, and begin the process of renewing our hearts and minds. There is a lot of information to learn, many skills to be developed, and action to be taken. We hope *What LIES Between Us* will not serve as your only source of engagement, but that you will use this to launch yourself into more profound and active work.

Please take your time going through the *What LIES Between Us* experience. We suggest that you complete the chapters in order and dedicate quality time to answering the reflective questions. Whether you are on your own or in a group, binge watching and reading the content—especially if this is all new to you—can take a toll on your emotional health.

If you are doing **What LIES Between Us** in a group setting, you will also engage in activities, and guided discussions that increase your capacity to engage in healing and life-giving conversations about race.

We have found that one of the most useful resources in helping to gain a fundamental understanding of race history, ideology, and impact is a three-episode series, produced by California Newsreel, called *Race-The Power of an Illusion*. This educational documentary investigates race in society, science, and history offering a great foundation for comprehending the mechanics of race.

Race-The Power of An Illusion, a three-part documentary is available a number of ways.

- Purchase at newsreel.org

- Borrow or stream from your local library

- Rent through Vimeo. Weekly ($2.99 per episode, $4.99 for the entire series).

ARE YOU DOING THIS STUDY ON YOUR OWN (NOT IN A GROUP)?

1. While watching the film, take notes writing down the information that is new to you. You will use your notes as you answer the reflective questions.

2. Once you completed all the assignments in one chapter, proceed to the next chapter.

ARE YOU DOING THIS STUDY IN A GROUP SETTING?

1. Watch one episode per meeting for three consecutive meetings.

2. While watching the film, take notes writing down the information that is new to you. You will use your notes as you answer the reflective questions, on your own, in your time away from the group.

3. After viewing an episode, if there is time, have a few people share only what they wrote down—the new information they learned, perhaps something that surprised them. This is not a good time to engage in a group discussion.

It is important to delay group discussion or dialogue until after you've completed all three episodes of the film. Why? Here is what we have discovered.

1. Early in your process, as a group, you may not have yet established the relational trust, respect, and security needed for vulnerable interactions. Having an unhealthy interaction at the beginning of your time together will more than likely result in people NOT returning to the group. Hopefully, after a few meetings, mutual trust, respect, and security between group members has formed.

2. Early in the journey, the tendency for self-centered, reactionary responses that stem from a lack of experience talking about race (like "I'm not racist," "I'm a good person," "Why can't we be colorblind?") are greater than after having completed chapters 1-4 of *What LIES Between Us*.

3. Significant to your journey toward unraveling race/ism is learning to listen, valuing the stories of others, learning to empathize, learning to see yourself as a contributor to a healing process, seeing yourself as a healer, not a debater.

By the time we are ready for a guided discussion, everyone in the group will have at least a common race education foundation and will have engaged in reflective thinking about the role race has played in shaping our beliefs and lives. We will have developed common awareness, understanding, and goals. Having completed this process as a group fosters the relational trust, respect and security needed to engage in constructive conversations. And we will have clarity and a vision for moving forward as the interdependent body and family that we truly are.

ARE YOU A GROUP FACILITATOR FOR THIS STUDY?

BEST PRACTICES

Place emphasis on the significance and importance of answering the questions in **Reflect-Rethink-Reach**. Introspection—examining your own mental and emotional processes—is extremely valuable to this process. During group discussions, you will notice a significant difference between those who are responding from self-analysis and those who have not and are only reacting to the information learned from the resources.

If your group needs less foundational material and wants more substantive content, additional resources are listed on our website, Brownicity.com. Also, doing a google search inclusive of the word, "syllabus" (e.g. "race syllabus") will most likely yield results for quality educational materials that have been well researched and documented. Avoid content that is propaganda and anecdotal commentary.

Take care to set up the physical meeting space to help foster a healing experience. For example, food, inspirational music, essential oil diffusion, and candles are a few things that help communicate and establish a good tone.

Also incorporating the arts or artistic expression helps to communicate the importance of our own power to create and encourages people to relax and enjoy becoming comfortable with an 'uncomfortable' topic. On our Brownicity You Tube channel, we feature a few vignettes of our artist-in-residence employing music and movement to help participants embody the lessons.

GROUP DISCUSSION MODEL

Once you complete the first five chapters, you will begin more group-oriented discussions and activities. At this time, you may want to review the Communication Triangle, Grace Space Guidelines and Common Language and Terms that will be introduced in chapter two.

You may also want to establish a "talking stick" type of method to encourage and support equal participation. We often remind participants that whoever has not completed their reflective journaling or any other "homework," should limit their engagement in group discussions to **listening**, only. We do this to support informed and reflective dialogue.

Do what works best for your group.

IMPORTANT TO NOTE:

What LIES Between Us is designed to help foster an experience to help us grow in our understanding of the race construct and how this stronghold has defiled our unity with each other and left us too fearful to confront it.

No part of this guide, journal or experience is intended to imply fault, blame, condemnation, or shame towards anyone or any people group. Shame and blame is not what we do! And we firmly believe and affirm that the "guilt-blame-shame" approach is never okay and is, in fact, counterproductive. Instead, we purpose to

- bring awareness and understanding,

- prompt us to challenge our beliefs, thoughts and actions that have contradicted our faith without us realizing it,

- help us unite against the LIES that have divided us,

- and equip and empower us to talk about race/ism, so that we can address and solve it.

Through ***What LIES Between Us*** and its recommended resources and activities, we hope to give you a foundation for further and deeper healing and exploration. Allow this to be a time of awakening, equipping, empowering, and growing your capacity to do justice. Wouldn't you love to be a part of the healing and restoration of individuals, families, communities, lives, and humanity?

❷
BELIEVE DIFFERENTLY

We cannot solve our problems with the same
thinking we used when we created them.
—Albert Einstein

Before we dive into content and discussions, it is important to our success that we set the tone. Let's be honest. No one is excited to jump into the race conversation. Race is seen as the dirty four letter word, the worst of all the dirty four-letter words. Just the mention of the word race can cause us to feel uncomfortable and anxious. And in many instances, when race has become a necessary part of our conversation, we recoil in defense ready to strike out in debate. It seems that somehow all by itself, the conversation on race turns volatile.

Well, we are not here to have THAT conversation on race—the one where folks feel compelled to debate, defend themselves, argue a political platform and drive the wedge of racial division deeper into hearts and minds. You see, we have inherited this very divisive way of addressing race from race itself—it is a lie and an ideology with a long standing legacy. Our adherence to race ideology has shaped us into opposition to oneness and fashioned us into weapons against each other.

But for healing to take place, we can no longer allow this ideology to use us as weapons against each other. Instead we have to allow ourselves—our beliefs and actions—to be shaped into instruments for love and justice. We cannot solve the problem of being divided by BEING DIVIDED. Through ***What LIES Between Us***, the conversation we will be having extends from the belief that we are ONE humanity.

In order to BE DIFFERENT, we must BELIEVE DIFFERENTLY!

Do not allow this world to mold you in its own image. Instead, be transformed from the inside out by renewing your mind. As a result, you will be able to discern what God wills and whatever God finds good, pleasing, and complete. Romans 12:2

Whether you are doing this study on your own or in a group, set the tone for a healing, life-giving, successful experience.

It is important that we honor the time and process for creating a space where you feel vulnerable enough to talk openly about race/ism. Some of us may have been given many opportunities to have open, constructive conversations about race and how it has affected us. Others of us may have been taught, directly or indirectly, to not talk about race. Because of this type of conversation gap, we will not rush into drudging through dense racial dialogue. Instead, we will take our time and build our capacity to engage with critical content and each other in healthy ways.

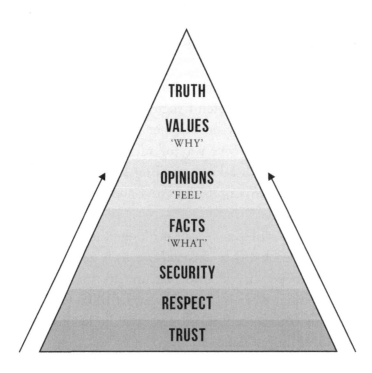

As shown in this communication triangle, we want to build upward, growing in our collective ability to engage in the truth—the truth about race and what seems to be true within us. In a group setting, we want to establish a **foundation** of **trust**, **respect**, and **security**. We can then build upon that foundation of trust, respect, and security to a **skill-based level** of communication where we can freely talk about **facts**, **opinions**, and **values** as we bring our personal stories to our group space. Likewise, the content will progress from **introductory foundational topics** like *melanin* and *genetics* to more complex skill based themes like *power* and *bias.*

Ultimately, our goal is to be able to communicate on a level of **truth**. Because many of us suffer from "race talk" anxiety and spend a lot of energy bracing ourselves for offenses and attacks, communicating truth in group settings rarely happens.

> *So put away your lies and speak the truth to one another because we are all part of one another.* Ephesians 4:25 (VOICE)

In a group setting, we will commit a significant amount of time establishing the foundation of trust, respect and security before moving up the triangle to communicating truth.

COMMON LANGUAGE & TERMS

Also important to successful communication is having a shared common language and a mutual understanding of terms and concepts related to race discourse. Because most of us have no formal education on race, we are unfamiliar with many essential terms and concepts. For example, many people have only addressed race/ism as a skin or moral issue. However, race/ism is a monstrous construct comprised of beliefs, power structures, politics, policies, disproportionalities, inequities, representations, biases, and much, much more. In order to deconstruct what race/ism has instilled in us, we have to be able to talk clearly and openly about all of its history, legacy, and levels. Essential terms and definitions are listed on our website, Brownicity.com.

GRACE SPACE GUIDELINES

If you are in a group setting, you will want to help foster and maintain an atmosphere where healing and growth can occur. Use these guidelines and keep them visible and within reach during group discussions.

1. **Listen.** Hear what is being shared. Be open to hearing perspectives and experiences that are different than yours.

2. **Respect and dignify.** Regard participants and their experiences as valuable and worthy of time and attention.

3. **Embrace discomfort.** It is okay to experience discomfort. The tension you feel now may be creating space for growth.

4. **Participate.** Engage in the activities and your journal. Speak up during meetings, but don't drown out the voices of others.

5. **Be free from guilt, shame, and condemnation.** Being socialized by race ideology is not a criminal offense.

6. **Use "I" not "we."** Avoid making statements that imply group representation. Speak about/for yourself, not "your people" or "those people."

7. **Avoid debating.** Back and forth personal debating indicates that someone is not listening and is counterproductive to contributing to a grace space.

8. **Keep a confidential table.** If someone in your group says something that upsets you, please don't call them out in public spaces.

9. **Focus on the USA.** For the sake of staying on task, limit your scope to the USA's issues.

10. **Respect the process.** There is no quick fix. The process consists of many steps and cycles—learning, lamenting, deconstructing, healing, restoring, building.

Also, keep in mind that depending on personal background and exposure to the race topic, each person in the group will have a different level of competence and capacity for engaging in this conversation. For example, a person who has a history of ascribing to "colorblindness" may take longer to adjust to an actual analysis of race than someone who has freely talked about race-related issues from childhood. Or a person for whom race has served as the crux of his/her identity may experience more of an emotional adjustment than someone who understands race to be a social and political construct. The diversity of experiences will be vast. In all cases, please practice being patient with each other.

NOTES

We have made space for you to write, draw, doodle, or take notes during our group experience.

Why are you engaging in *What LIES Between Us*?

What are you seeking?

REFLECT RETHINK REACH

Complete this portion of **Reflect—Rethink—Reach**.

REFLECT

1. Regarding thinking/talking about and socializing around race, where are you? Where would you like to be?

2. How does talking about race make you feel?

3. Do you talk about race in your home and with friends?

4. How comfortable are you talking about race? How comfortable are you with talking about race with children?

5. How and how often do you address issues of racial inequality?

6. Do you find it difficult to address race related issues in your family?

7. Typically, what prompts your thoughts or discussions about race?

8. Do you explore and/or challenge your own racial reality?

9. Do you attempt to understand people whose ethnic background is different from yours?

10. Do you intentionally develop relationships with people outside of your ethnic and cultural group? What are your thoughts on doing this?

11. Are there places that you frequent where you are the racial or ethnic minority (e.g. school, church, organizations, activities)? Are you a decision maker there?

12. What actions do you take to encourage and support unity?

REFLECTIVE JOURNALING

Write down your thoughts.

1. Why have you embarked on this journey towards healing and restoration?

2. What do you hope to gain?

3. If you could create your hearts desire, what would the world look like? For example, what do you foresee as inalienable rights for individuals, family, community, etc? If you had the right to pursue happiness, what would you do?

4. What is keeping you from doing what you described for question 3?

If you are in a group:

5. What was the common theme extrapolated from your meeting?

6. What is the theme showing you?

RETHINK

1. Identify healing and life-giving words that you've heard or used in conversations about race. When you say these, words, how do they make you feel?

2. Now identify hurtful and angry words that you've heard or used in conversations about race. When you say these, words, how do they make you feel?

3. Say to yourself, 'I am a creative conductor. It is up to me to help transform a *cacophony* into *consonance.*'

   cacophony—loud, confused, discordant, jarring and usually inharmonious noise; a harsh, discordant mixture of sounds.

   consonance—the combination of notes that are in harmony with each other due to the relationship between their frequencies.

4. Think about how you talk about race. Do people feel as though they can be vulnerable and ask you "stupid" questions?

5. What have you gathered about what it takes to create, engage in, and sustain healthy environments for healing and change?

6. How might you respond to someone who wants to get into a personal debate about race?

7. How might you respond when a friend or family member makes a racist comment?

REACH

WHAT DOES LOVE SOUND LIKE?

When we talk about race/ism, we don't want to contribute to the cacophony of popular race rhetoric that seems to be the norm. We don't want to fan the flames of the molotov cocktail of personal, political, and religious perspectives void of historical context and full of emotional vomiting, systemically unaware news coverage of race-related events, and motives void of nurturing understanding, healing, and unity! We refuse to engage in a way that adds to the fear, anxiety, hopelessness, pain, and injustice that exhausts us all.

We consider our contribution to the healing process and we ask ourselves, "Are my thoughts and actions helpful, hopeful, inspiring and encouraging? Am I contributing to healing and change?" We do our homework. We do our research. We recognize race ideology as the GIANT ENEMY and people as victims of its deception, legacy and intimidation! WE WILL NOT SLING ROCKS AT PEOPLE!

As we build our capacity to engage in courageous conversations and living in the chasm of racial division, WE WILL BE CREATORS of safe spaces where people can be transparent and vulnerable. Inspired and sustained by love, such spaces cultivate healing and change that overflow into the lives of those around us. And that's what we are going for. Because when race/ism is addressed in the context of love, it loses its power!

—*Lucretia C. Berry (brownicity.com, 2015)*

MEDITATE

Don't use foul or abusive language. Let everything you say be good and helpful, so that your words will be an encouragement to those who hear them. Ephesians 4:29 NLT

Some people make cutting remarks, but the words of the wise bring healing. Proverbs 12:18 NLT

What if I speak in the most elegant languages of people or in the exotic languages of the heavenly messengers, but I live without love? Well then, anything I say is like the clanging of brass or a crashing cymbal. What if I have the gift of prophecy, am blessed with knowledge and insight to all the mysteries, or what if my faith is strong enough to scoop a mountain from its bedrock, yet I live without love? If so, I am nothing. I could give all that I have to feed the poor, I could surrender my body to be burned as a martyr, but if I do not live in love, I gain nothing by my selfless acts. Love is patient; love is kind. Love isn't envious, doesn't boast, brag, or strut about. There's no arrogance in love; it's never rude, crude, or indecent—it's not self-absorbed. Love isn't easily upset. Love doesn't tally wrongs or celebrate injustice; but truth—yes, truth—is love's delight! Love puts up with anything and everything that comes along; it trusts, hopes, and endures no matter what. Love will never become obsolete. I Corinthians 13:1-8 VOICE

PRAYER

May we begin to see ourselves and each other in the image You have created — *Imago Dei.** Thank You for guiding us through continued transformation.

*Imago Dei - image of God.

❸
RACE, GENETICS & BIOLOGY

WATCH:
Race-The Power of an Illusion
Episode 1 - The Difference Between Us
This episode examines the contemporary science -
including genetics - that challenges our common
sense assumptions that human beings can be bundled
into three or four fundamentally different groups
according to their physical traits.

While watching the film, take notes. Write down the information that is new for you. You will use your notes to complete this chapter's portion of **Reflect—Rethink—Reach**.

SUGGESTED GROUP ACTIVITY

1. Before watching the film, identify someone who you perceive is the most like you. Write down their name and why.

2. After watching the film, reflect on your choice and if you now think differently based on what you learned in the film.

NOTES

Film Notes. Write down the information that is new for you.

Complete this portion of **Reflect—Rethink—Reach**.

REFLECT

Review the new information you learned from watching *The Difference Between Us*.

1. Did you learn something new? Review what you wrote down while watching the documentary. Do you want this information to be part of your understanding about race?

2. What beliefs did you have about the biology of race before watching the film?

3. Is there dissonance between what you learned in the film and what you thought you knew about lack of genetic differences?

4. How did what you learned from the film make you feel (e.g. uncomfortable, relieved, confused, etc.)?

5.   Where did your previous knowledge of race come from?

6.   What information about race do you choose to believe—what you knew prior to watching the film or what the film presented?

REFLECTIVE JOURNALING

Write down your thoughts. LOOK at them. SEE where you need to change your beliefs and thinking.

How were your beliefs about the "biology" of race established?

1. Identify stories or narratives, social, cultural, political and religious messages and traditions, history lessons, teachings, anecdotes, personal experiences, etc. through which wrong information about genetic differences was communicated. Write about some of those here.

2. Now write how you have benefited from the false belief you internalized. Then, write how you have suffered.

3. What feelings were rooted in your belief about genetic differences (e.g. pride, superiority, inferiority, entitlement, victimization, shame, anger, guilt)? Write them down.

4. Identify decisions you have made based on these feelings. Write them down.

RETHINK

1. Hitler's ideology about racial superiority was thwarted by Jesse Owens' olympic victory. But instead of abandoning his beliefs, Hitler and other eugenicists sought other measures to reinforce it. Why? Were your beliefs about the biology of race challenged by what you learned in this film? If so, will you abandon your beliefs or come up with ways to justify them?

2. Ask yourself: Does my belief in the "biology" of race keep me from seeing people as fully human? Do my beliefs rob people of value and dignity? Instead, do I see them as a part of a racial, social, or political category (e.g. white, black, latino, thug, poor, ghetto, rich, liberal, conservative)?

3. Does my belief align or conflict with Genesis 1:27 NLT? How so?

   So God created human beings in his own image. In the image of God he created them; male and female he created them.

4. Now revisit your decisions and feelings that you wrote down. Would they be different if you actually believed Genesis 1:27 and what you learned in the film?

5. What have you been taught about your feelings that are rooted in what you believed about the "biology" of race (e.g. pride, superiority, inferiority, entitlement, victimization, shame, anger, guilt)?

MEDITATE

Don't copy the behavior and customs of this world, but let God transform you into a new person by changing the way you think. Then you will learn to know God's will for you, which is good and pleasing and perfect. Romans 12:2 VOICE

ASK YOURSELF

By believing in the biology of race, have I copied the behavior and customs of the world?

REACH

A belief in race is no more sound than believing that the sun revolves around the earth, or that the earth is flat, but it has become so deeply embedded in our psyches and so widely accepted.

How will you continue to move forward with a renewed mind? What do you need to do? Practice new thoughts? Actively disconnect from false beliefs? Forgive sources of false beliefs (e.g. parents, community, school, country)? Engage in resources offering truth?

MEDITATE

But whenever someone turns to the Lord, the veil is taken away. For the Lord is the Spirit, and wherever the Spirit of the Lord is, there is freedom. So all of us who have had that veil removed can see and reflect the glory of the Lord. And the Lord—who is the Spirit—makes us more and more like him as we are changed into his glorious image. 2 Corinthians 3:16 NLT

We are human, but we don't wage war as humans do. We use God's mighty weapons, not worldly weapons, to knock down the strongholds of human reasoning and to destroy false arguments. We destroy every proud obstacle that keeps people from knowing God. We capture their rebellious thoughts and teach them to obey Christ. 2 Corinthians 10:3-5 NLT

PRAYER

Lord, I am grateful for your desire and provision for me to be FREE—free from beliefs that deceive and oppress me, my family and neighbors and prohibit us from reflecting the fullness of your glory. In, by, and through You, I am pulling down false beliefs that oppose your character and truth. Help me to do whatever it takes to change and walk in a renewed identity—a reflection of Your Glorious Image.

④
A LIE PERPETUATED

WATCH:
Race-The Power of an Illusion
Episode 2 - The Story We Tell

This episode uncovers the roots of the race concept in North America, the 19th century science that legitimated it, and how it came to be held so fiercely in the western imagination. The episode is an eye-opening tale of how race served to rationalize, even justify, American social inequalities as "natural."

While watching the film, take notes. Write down the information that is new for you. You will use your notes to complete this chapter's portion of **Reflect—Rethink—Reach**.

SUGGESTED GROUP DISCUSSION

If there is time after watching the film, briefly share and discuss some of the themes that emerged from your note taking. Here are a few sample topics:

> Why is it socially acceptable to identify Hitler's behavior of 'superiority' as psychotic but not include Jefferson, Adams, Morton, and other early American leaders in that category?

Why do we find it acceptable for people with economic and political power to engage in criminal activity such as murder, theft, and breach of contract? Why are poor people not afforded that same 'hero' status for committing those same types of crimes?

NOTES

Film Notes. Write down the information that is new for you.

Complete this portion of **Reflect—Rethink—Reach**.

REFLECT

Review the new information you learned from watching *The Story We Tell*.

1. Did you learn something new? Review what you wrote down while watching the documentary. Do you want this information to be part of your understanding about race?

2. How did what you learned from the film make you feel (e.g. uncomfortable, relieved, confused, etc.)?

3. How have you assigned meaning to how people look?

4. How do you feel about Thomas Jefferson's role in securing the race narrative?

5. To justify treating them inhumanely and disregard their human rights, Cherokees were vilified or criminalized. How do we vilify and criminalize people today?

6. Do we still expect people to fit into the ideals of "civilization" that were shaped by these hundreds years old ideas?

7. The "white man's burden" inspired Americans to perceive "uncivilized" nations as people they could "bring along" or "advance in civilization?" In what ways does the inspiration for USA Christian missions work correlate with the 'white mans burden?'

REFLECTIVE JOURNALING

Write down your thoughts. LOOK at them. SEE where you need to change your beliefs and thoughts.

1. How many **LIES** has the race narrative told you? Name them. Count them. Write them down. Now replace the lie with the truth. Because the race narrative is so pervasive in our culture, you can not count and name all of its **LIES**. But identifying some will open the door for others to be identified and deconstructed.

2. Now write how you have benefited from the lie. Then, write how you have suffered from the lie.

3. What feelings were rooted in your belief in the race narrative (e.g. pride, superiority, inferiority, entitlement, victimization, shame, anger, guilt)? Write them down.

4. Identify decisions you have made based on these feelings. Write them down.

5. How has the race narrative influenced your beliefs about who you are and your role in society? Why is it important to know and understand this?

RETHINK

1. Do your personal values about equality, justice, peace and unity conflict or coincide with the race narrative? How so?

2. Is your personal identity tied to the race narrative? Explain.

3. How do you interpret Ephesians 2:11-22 (VOICE)?

> *So never forget how you used to be. Those of you born as outsiders to Israel were outcasts, branded "the uncircumcised" by those who bore the sign of the covenant in their flesh, a sign made with human hands. You had absolutely no connection to the Anointed; you were strangers, separated from God's people. You were aliens to the covenant they had with God; you were hopelessly stranded without God in a fractured world. But now, because of Jesus the Anointed and His sacrifice, all of that has changed. God gathered you who were so far away and brought you near to Him by the royal blood of the Anointed, our Liberating King.*
>
> *He is the embodiment of our peace, sent once and for all to take down the great barrier of hatred and hostility that has divided us so that we can be one. He offered His body on the sacrificial altar to bring an end to the law's ordinances and dictations that separated Jews from the outside nations. His desire was to create in His body one new humanity from the two opposing groups, thus creating peace. Effectively the cross becomes God's means to kill off the hostility once and for all so that He is able to reconcile them both to God in this one new body.*
>
> *The Great Preacher of peace and love came for you, and His voice found those of you who were near and those who were far away. By Him both have access to the Father in one Spirit. And so you are no longer called outcasts and wanderers but citizens with God's people, members of God's holy family, and residents of His household. You are being built on a solid foundation: the message of the prophets and the voices of God's chosen emissaries[a] with Jesus, the Anointed Himself, the precious cornerstone. The building is joined together stone by stone—all of us chosen and sealed in Him, rising up to become a holy temple in the Lord. In Him you are being built together, creating a sacred dwelling place among you where God can live in the Spirit.*

4. Are there any words or phrases that stand out to you?

5. Does the race ideology or narrative work within the "oneness and peace" described in these verses? When does the race narrative override the "oneness and peace" described in these verses?

Meditate on 2 Corinthians 10:3-6 (MES) and recognize the power you have in Christ for challenging systems within and around you.

The world is unprincipled. It's dog-eat-dog out there! The world doesn't fight fair. But we don't live or fight our battles that way— never have and never will. The tools of our trade aren't for marketing or manipulation, but they are for demolishing that entire massively corrupt culture. We use our powerful God-tools for smashing warped philosophies, tearing down barriers erected against the truth of God, fitting every loose thought and emotion and impulse into the structure of life shaped by Christ. Our tools are ready at hand for clearing the ground of every obstruction and building lives of obedience into maturity.

Meditate on Romans 12:2 (MES) and invite transformation to take place.

So here's what I want you to do, God helping you: Take your everyday, ordinary life—your sleeping, eating, going-to-work, and walking-around life—and place it before God as an offering. Embracing what God does for you is the best thing you can do for him. Don't become so well-adjusted to your culture that you fit into it without even thinking. Instead, fix your attention on God. You'll be changed from the inside out. Readily recognize what he wants from you, and quickly respond to it. Unlike the culture around you, always dragging you down to its level of immaturity, God brings the best out of you, develops well-formed maturity in you.

REACH

1. How will you actively disconnect from the race narrative? Will you engage in more resources to learn more about the race construct? Will you forgive sources of false beliefs (e.g. church, parents, community, school, country)?

2. Do you need to seek forgiveness for surrendering to the race lie and perpetuating it?

> *If we confess our sins, He is faithful and just to forgive us our sins and to cleanse us from all unrighteousness.*
> 1 John 1:9 NIV

MEDITATE

But whenever someone turns to the Lord, the veil is taken away. For the Lord is the Spirit, and wherever the Spirit of the Lord is, there is freedom. So all of us who have had that veil removed can see and reflect the glory of the Lord. And the Lord—who is the Spirit— makes us more and more like him as we are changed into his glorious image. 2 Corinthians 3:16-18 NLT

We are human, but we don't wage war as humans do. We use God's mighty weapons, not worldly weapons, to knock down the strongholds of human reasoning and to destroy false arguments. We destroy every proud obstacle that keeps people from knowing God. We capture their rebellious thoughts and teach them to obey Christ. 2 Corinthians 10:3-5 NLT

PRAYER

Lord, I am grateful for your desire and provision for me to be FREE—free from beliefs that deceive and oppress me, my family and neighbors and prohibit us from reflecting the fullness of your glory. In, by, and through You, I am pulling down false beliefs that oppose your character and truth. Help me to do whatever it takes to change and walk in a renewed identity—a reflection of Your Glorious Image.

❺
THE PROFIT OF RACE

WATCH:
Race-The Power of an Illusion
Episode 3 - The House We Live In

If race is not biology, what is it? This episode uncovers how race resides not in nature but in politics, economics and culture. It reveals how our social institutions "make" race by disproportionately channeling resources, power, status, and wealth to white people.

While watching the film, take notes. Write down the information that is new for you. You will use your notes to complete this chapter's portion of **Reflect—Rethink—Reach**.

NOTES

Film Notes. Write down the information that is new for you.

Complete this portion of **Reflect—Rethink—Reach**.

REFLECT

Review the new information you learned from watching *The House We Live In*.

1. Did you learn something new? Review what you wrote down while watching the documentary. Do you want this information to be part of your understanding about 'how race is made?'

2. How does what you learned in the film make you feel? Are you experiencing any hurt, anger, grief, or sorrow? It is healthy to pause, acknowledge these emotions and express your lament. Lamenting is when we release our grief and sorrow, which creates space for and invites healing and restoration.

3. If you completed the documentary, you have learned how race has an intricate relationship with wealth and poverty. Why are people poor? Do you believe that poor people do not succeed because they are lazy?

4. *Meritocracy* refers to a social system in which individuals advance and earn reward in direct proportion to their individual abilities and efforts. What do you think about meritocracy? What is the relationship between a race-based system and a merit-based system?

5. History, policies, systems and structures underscore racial injustices and division and are beyond the control of any one individual. Do you tend to blame individuals for systemic and structural problems? Do you believe that only the individual needs to change in order for systemic and structural problems to improve?

6. Our social institutions **"make"** race by disproportionately channeling resources, power, status and wealth to white people. Do you believe that there are advantages to being white in our racial system? Do you believe that there are disadvantages to being a person of color in this system?

7. Had you heard of the term "block busting?" How do you feel about banks and real estate agencies preying on the racial- and economic-based fears of white people? What other agencies and institutions do this to get you to make decisions in their best interests?

8. Have you attributed the conditions of ghettos, "sketchy" neighborhoods, urban and low-income areas solely to the individuals that live in them? Whether you live there or drive through, do you ever think about how these areas were **"made"**?

9. Are you complicit with the economic and social disparities in our country? Why or why not?

REFLECTIVE JOURNALING

Write down your thoughts. LOOK at them. SEE where you need to change your beliefs and thinking.

1. What year did your American ancestors gain citizenship? What year were they granted the right to vote?

2. How have your family dynamics played into how you have thought about race ?

3. What are the stories that you have been told about the shortcomings and problems of poor people?

4. What are the stories that you have been told about wealth? What have you been told about 'job creators and makers' and 'job and resource takers?'

5. The post WWII housing crunch, white flight, and blockbusting occurred in recent history. How do these events relate to you personally? What is your story? How were you or someone you know affected? How have you benefited from these events? How were you disadvantaged by these events?

6. Many institutions use our fear to manipulate us into making decisions in their best interest. Have you allowed feelings about race (e.g. pride, fear, superiority, inferiority, entitlement, victimization, shame, anger, guilt) determine where you "do life"—reside, school, church, friends, social activities? Explain.

RETHINK

History, policies, systems, structures, and false beliefs underscore racial injustices and discord. Ask yourself:

1. Am I complicit with this? What am I doing to perpetuate this? What am I doing to dismantle this?

2. Do my personal values about justice, peace, unity, "loving my neighbor" coincide or conflict with racial discord and injustices? How so?

3. Justice flowed from the essence of Jesus.
   - with Samaritans as expressed in John 4:9

   - with women as expressed in John 4:27

   - with tax collectors and those classed as "sinners" as expressed in Matthew 9:10-12, Mark 2:15-17, Luke 5:29-31

   - with the Gentiles (people of a different faith) as expressed in Matthew 15:21-28, Mark 7:24-29

Like the people described in these passages, you can probably relate to needing Jesus' justice. But don't you also want justice to flow from you as it did Jesus?

Meditate on 2 Corinthians 10:3-5 (VOICE) and recognize the power you have in Christ for challenging systems within and around you.

> *For though we walk in the world, we do not fight according to this world's rules of warfare. The weapons of the war we're fighting are not of this world but are powered by God and effective at tearing down the strongholds erected against His truth. We are demolishing arguments and ideas, every high-and-mighty philosophy that pits itself against the knowledge of the one true God. We are taking prisoners of every thought, every emotion, and subduing them into obedience to the Anointed One.*

Meditate on Romans 12:2 (VOICE) and invite transformation to take place.

> *Do not allow this world to mold you in its own image. Instead, be transformed from the inside out by renewing your mind. As a result, you will be able to discern what God wills and whatever God finds good, pleasing, and complete.*

REACH

In Mark 7, Jesus challenges the scribes and pharisees when they fail to see how their religious traditions get in the way of God's commands. He tells them,

> *Do you think God wants you to honor your traditions that you have passed down? This is only one of many places where you are blind.* (v13 VOICE)

Sadly, our traditional Sunday worship services are referred to as the most segregated time of the week in our country. The church strongly reflects the political and social construct of race. But as followers of Jesus Christ, we should be a reflection of Him.

We will not allow our traditions—history, policies, systems, structures, false beliefs—to compromise God's vision for justice, peace, joy love and oneness. We will no longer be blind to the political and social construct of race ! Are you willing to help make this invisible system visible?

In Romans 15, Paul talks about how corporate responsibility requires that we make personal sacrifices for the sake of our brothers and sisters. He offers the example of Jesus who gave up His life for the sake of the world. Living by this ethic, what will you sacrifice to foster healing and change? (e.g. comfort, ego, ethnocentrism, racial allegiance, control, status, love of money, status, friends, popularity, people pleasing, etc).

1. How will you continue to move forward with the process of being transformed?

2. How will you actively engage in transforming your family, church, community? What specific steps will you take?

3. Will you find it especially difficult to move forward with transformation in your family and community? How so?

MEDITATE

But in the moment when one turns toward the Lord, the veil is removed. By "the Lord" what I mean is the Spirit, and in any heart where the Spirit of the Lord is present, there is liberty. Now all of us, with our faces unveiled, reflect the glory of the Lord as if we are mirrors; and so we are being transformed, metamorphosed, into His same image from one radiance of glory to another, just as the Spirit of the Lord accomplishes it.
2 Corinthians 3:16-18 VOICE

PRAYER

Lord, I am grateful for your desire and provision for me to be FREE—free from beliefs that deceive and oppress me, my family and neighbors and prohibit us from reflecting the fullness of your glory. In, by, and through You, I am pulling down false beliefs that oppose your character and truth. Help me to do whatever it takes to change and walk in a renewed identity—a reflection of Your Glorious Image. Direct me in what comes next as you continue to transform me to help transform my family and community.

ARE YOU DOING THIS STUDY IN A GROUP SETTING?

As you expand into more group-oriented discussions and activities, recall the Communication Triangle, Grace Space Guidelines (chapter one), and essential Terms (Brownicity.com) for communicating clearly.

You may also want to establish a "talking stick" type of method to encourage and support equal participation. We often remind participants that whoever has not completed their reflective journaling or any other "homework," should limit their engagement in group discussions to **listening**, only. We do this to encourage informed and reflective dialogue.

Do what works best for your group.

❻
DISRUPTING LIES, LIVING TRUTH

The truth may hurt for a little while but a lie hurts forever.
— Anonymous.

In recent history, one of the biggest LIES we've come to believe about race is that if we don't talk about race, racism will end. Instead, silence, lack of race education, and pretending not to see color have left us void of language, power, and permission to collectively dismantle racism. And furthermore, our adherence to these LIES has fueled the preservation of race/ism. Does *not* talking about cancer heal cancer? Does *not* talking about human trafficking end human trafficking? Bringing attention to a disease, whether personal or social, doesn't cause more suffering. Instead, spotlighting the disorder mobilizes us toward ending the suffering, seeking a cure, and establishing preventative measures.

Let's TALK about race!

Let's disrupt the LIES!

Let's live the truth!

Have you watched the documentary in its entirety?

Have you engaged in your journal?

Did you check out any of the other related resources at brownicity.com? If so, which ones?

The documentary covered a broad scope of race history. If you haven't already, research and identify how race has been "made"—shaped by disproportionately channeling resources, power, wealth, and status to white people—in the community in which you currently live. In other words, what is the race history of your neighborhood, city, and/or county?

Where do you see yourself in the local race story?

ACTIVITY

This activity can be used for personal reflection or group discussion.

Spend some time debriefing about what you gained from the documentary and reflective journaling.

1. Share something notable that you discovered about yourself so far?

2. Was there a point where you grieved? What bothered you or left you unsettled?

3. Was there a point where you were relieved? Did you discover something that brought clarity to your perspective on race ?

4. How has your thinking changed about race/ism? Did you have an "ah ha" moment? Share how you believe or think differently than you did before.

5. Share a personal story from your reflective journaling.

NOTES

Complete this portion of **Reflect—Rethink—Reach**.

REFLECT

1. Were you ever shamed into not talking about race?

2. Do you have shame associated with your 'racial identity?'

3. What was the common theme extrapolated from completing this chapter's activities?

4. What is this theme showing you?

5. If you are in a group, what impacted you from your group time?

6. What was the common theme extrapolated from your meeting?

7. What is this theme showing you?

REFLECTIVE JOURNALING

Identify a race lie, false narrative, or story that you believed. Rewrite or record the truth.

RETHINK

1. How do you define peace? Does talking about race break peace
    or make peace?

2. What have you assumed?

3. What do you believe to be true?

REACH

Before starting the next chapter (and/or the next group meeting), do
the following.

1. Watch the **Implicit Association Video**. The link is listed at
    Brownicity.com or you can do a google search for "Harvard
    Implicit Bias Test."

2. Take the test labeled, "race (Black-White IAT)."

3. Write down your test results (e.g. "moderate bias toward European-American").

4. How do you feel about your Implicit Association Test results?

5. What is the correlation between your test results and race ideology?

MEDITATION AND PRAYER
May we be people of peace,
With voices of hope,
Doing the hard work of love.

❼
REPRESENTATION, STEREOTYPES & BIAS

Use your mind…or someone else will.
— David Hallett

There are forces that have shaped our national consciousness by writing many of us out of the human family and leaving the rest of us to function without a societal mirror. Decision-makers and media representatives systematically reframe our history to cultivate fear and ignorance. Fear and ignorance are a perfect recipe for feeding the narratives that subtly seduce us into indifference to racism, segregation, poverty, genocide, and the list of dehumanization goes on. The consequences have been reprehensible, disgraceful, and seemingly unforgivable.

BUT as we take on the responsibility of becoming aware, we are empowered to reject the frames, narratives, and subliminal messages that have lied to us and robbed us all of human dignity.

ACTIVITY 1

These questions can be prompts for personal reflection or group discussion.

1. Did you watch the Implicit Association Video and take the test?

2. What were your test results (e.g. "moderate bias toward European-American")?

3. How do you feel about your Implicit Association test results?

4. What is the correlation between your test results and race ideology?

ACTIVITY 2

This activity can be used for personal reflection or group discussion.

Historically, the objectives and language for securing a race-based social hierarchy were overtly expressed, widely accepted, and celebrated. Today, these ideals are openly criticized, but the legacy is still in play in more covert ways. Do you recognize current "coded" objectives and language used in media, marketing, and politics?

Watch any of the videos listed for this section (Brownicity.com) and talk about the relationship between media representation, stereotypes, and implicit bias—how and why they are formed and sustained.

1. What forces are shaping our national conscious?
   Are these neutral influences?

2. Whose interests are being served?

3. Examine how your own identity has been shaped and framed by certain racial narratives and messages. How do you identify yourself? How is your identity tied to race ? Is race the primary source of your identity? Does race narrate your identity or determine what choices you make?

4. What are the dangers of media representation, stereotypes, and implicit bias as they relate to profiling?

5. Give an example of a frame, narrative, and message that has influenced you regarding race? *Moving the Race Conversation Forward* resource listed at Brownicity.com provides insight into 'frames, narratives and messages.'

6. Name a few micro-aggressions that you have said, heard, or experienced and identify what makes them offensive.

GROUP ACTIVITY

CHANGE THE NARRATIVE CAMPAIGN

Watch the videos listed for this section at Brownicity.com. The relationship between media representation, stereotypes, and implicit bias is clear. In your group, create a campaign to disrupt, change, or reverse one of the narratives disclosed in the videos or a harmful narrative that has strongly influenced and shaped your local community.

As you create your campaign, consider the following:

- The target audience for your campaign

- Your goal

- The message that will help you meet your goal

- The strategies you will use

REFLECT RETHINK REACH

Complete this portion of **Reflect—Rethink—Reach**.

REFLECT

1. What was the common theme extrapolated from completing this chapter's activities?

2. What is this theme showing you?

3. If you are in a group, what impacted you from your group time?

4. What was the common theme extrapolated from your meeting?

5. What is this theme showing you?

REFLECTIVE JOURNALING

Identify a time where you now recognize that your implicit racial bias was at work without you knowing it.

RETHINK

Our subconscious beliefs, not necessarily the beliefs we profess, dictate our conscious life. If you've been honest and transparent with yourself, you've identified areas in your life where 'invisible' forces of racial conditioning have heavily influenced your thoughts and actions.

Is this what you want?

REACH

Until unconscious bias becomes conscious unbiased, I will speak out.
—Kim Honeycutt

Choose to be ACTIVE in reshaping your conscious and our national conscious.

Choose to SEE what has seemed invisible.

Choose to do the work of RENEWING your mind.

Before starting the next chapter (and/or the next group meeting), listen to the podcast, *This American Life: The Problem We All Live With* (50 minutes). The link can be found at Brownicity.com.

MEDITATION AND PRAYER

May we be people of peace,
With voices of hope,
Doing the hard work of love.

❽
POWER, POLICIES & PEOPLE

*To show compassion for an individual without
showing concern for the structures
of society that make him an object of compassion
is to be sentimental rather than loving.*
— *William Sloane Coffin*

Often our scope of addressing race is limited to a critique of individuals and group culture. Meanwhile, our examination fails to investigate and question the impact and influence of systems and a larger culture at work. Let's borrow from this wonderful fish bowl analogy.

There are two fish bowls—one dirty and one clean. You see an obvious difference between the water in each bowl. Are you concerned about the fish having to swim in a polluted bowl? Do you ask how the polluted fishbowl got that way? Do you blame the fish for the polluted fishbowl water? Do you focus on "cleaning" the fish and put it back into the dirty water? Do you clean the water?

Often, we look at a person's or community's social and economic inequities or unfortunate outcomes and then indulge in an ineffectual and erroneous campaign for judging those individuals and communities as solely responsible for the outcomes. In other words, we condemn individuals or communities for conditions largely established by systems. This toxic interpretation often fuels toxic beliefs about people and communities.

Let's further explore how **systemic racism*** (institutional and structural) thrives and reinforces **individual racism*** (internalized and interpersonal) which in turn helps to preserve systemic racism, and the cycle continues.

ACTIVITY 1

This activity can be used for personal reflection or group discussion.

1.   Did you listen to the podcast, *This American Life: The Problem We All Live With?*

2.   Did you see yourself anywhere in this story? Which person or people did you most closely relate to or identify with? Why?

*Review *Common Language and Terms* (Chapter 2 at brownicity.com)

3. Identify systemic racism at work. Is it overt or covert?

4. Identify individual racism at work. Is it overt or covert?

Now, let's do a **power analysis**—an examination of the intersections between power, policies, and people. Here are a few things to keep in mind.

- Politically and economically motivated operations have sociopolitical implications.

- With every decision made, someone is advantaged and someone is disadvantaged.

When doing a power analysis, ask and answer these questions.

- Who makes the rules?

- Who created the standard?

- Who is impacted?

- How are advantaged people perceived, received, and believed?

- How are disadvantaged people perceived, received, and believed? (Adapted from Dr. Jewell Cooper, UNC Greensboro School of Education).

1. In this podcast scenario, who is responsible? What role does each of the following play in shaping outcomes:

    •   Individuals?

    •   Society and culture?

    •   Systemic structures?

2. Who has decision-making authority?

3. Who has power?

4. In this context, how does the principle, 'Be hard on systems and soft on people' apply?

ACTIVITY 2

This activity can be used for personal reflection or group discussion.

As shown in the podcast, *This American Life: The Problem We All Live With?*, race/ism has a role for everyone. What roles have you played? What's your story? Share your story with a partner, perhaps someone who may have experienced race differently than you. Listen carefully to your partner's story. Think about all the forces that may have shaped your partner's story. Hear their story in context.

During your time of reflective journaling, write a healing and helpful response to your partner's story.

Or one person can share their compelling story as the group listens. Then each group member will write a healing and helpful response to that one story during his/her time of reflective journaling.

NOTES

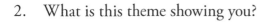

Complete this portion of **Reflect—Rethink—Reach**.

REFLECT

1. What was the common theme extrapolated from completing this chapter's activities?

2. What is this theme showing you?

3. If you are in a group, what impacted you from your group time?

4. What was the common theme extrapolated from your meeting?

5. What is this theme showing you?

REFLECTIVE JOURNALING

Write a response to someone's story that supports the value of their story. Do not justify or explain away their story. Take the time to connect to their story—find meaning in their story. Practice being a healing and life-giving source for those who express trauma and brokenness due to racism.

RETHINK

Decades of research have noted the impact of discrimination and racism on the psychological health of communities of color. Read ***Racial Trauma Is Real***. The link can be found at Brownicity.com.

REACH

Think about how you can help heal racial trauma instead of contributing to it, ignoring it, or explaining it away. If you have or you know someone who has experienced racial trauma, identify healing steps to take.

MEDITATION AND PRAYER

May we be people of peace,
With voices of hope,
Doing the hard work of love.

⑨
AFTER AMEN

*I can't know how God feels about our 'thoughts and prayers.' But I
am positive God would be far more pleased if we would open our eyes,
lift up our heads, get up off our knees, and go and do something.*
—Rev. James C. Howell
(Its Time for the End to Our Prayers, July 8, 2016*)*

What if, instead of having forced, sporadic race conversations prompted by the news media's broadcast of catastrophic events, we were fluent and proficient in the language and practice of anti-racism? What if you had grown up with knowledge and understanding about how race works? What if you had been equipped, empowered, and inspired as a child to become the best anti-racist ever or a leader in dismantling racism and racial healing. What if everywhere you turned—school, sports, profession, church—racial healing and justice was a priority?

With all kinds of initiatives, efforts, programs, ministries, therapy, etc. in place to help heal from the devastation of disease, broken relationships, addiction, shame, abuse, and human trafficking, we know that taking action is essential. Simply feeling sympathy for the brokenness does not advance the healing process.

ACTIVITY

Read ***It's Time for the End to our Prayers***. The link can be found at brownicity.com.

Racism affects just about every aspect of our lives—education, heath care, housing, opportunities (determined by policies), and the justice system. In order to heal and change our communities, we have to address racism outright.

Discuss and explore how you will move forward with intention. How will you contribute to healing and change? in your life? family? community? personally, socially, and politically?

Here are a few prompts.

1. How will you practice change?

2. Where is your influence (e.g. home, neighborhood, school, church, hobbies, etc)? How can you use your influence in these areas?

3. What can you offer?

4. How are you talking to your children about race ?

5. How will you help restore what race/ism has broken?

6. What are you afraid of?

7. What do you see as challenges?

Here are a few ideas for things you can do.

1. Commit to learning more. Name twelve people you can invite to join you. Include children.

2. Lead a book study or a group that helps equip and empower folks for healing and change?

3. Join or connect with groups—local, online, etc—actively engaged in the work.

4. Commit to intentionally growing relationships with friends who are ethnically different than you. You could

    *   invite them over to your home for dinner,

    *   go to their house for dinner, or

    *   become a member of a different community—one that takes you outside of your racial comfort zone (e.g. sports team, church, fitness group)

State what you will do.

I WILL
*   read (watch, listen to)
*   talk to
*   research
*   join
*   change
*   practice
*   stop
*   start
*   continue
*   sign up for
*   attend
*   host
*   lead
*   volunteer for/at

NOTES

Complete this portion of **Reflect—Rethink—Reach**.

1. What was the common theme extrapolated from completing this chapter's activities?

2. What is this theme showing you?

3. If you are in a group, what impacted you from your group time?

4. What was the common theme extrapolated from your meeting?

5. What is this theme showing you?

REFLECTIVE JOURNALING

Write your vision and goals for contributing to healing and change. What specifically will you do?

Push yourself to reach beyond where you are now. Having conversations, no matter how informed, is not enough. You must engage in transformative action.

RETHINK

The perception of power is our own understanding of our ability
to change our environment.
—Eric Law
(quoted in Brenda Salter McNeil's *Roadmap to Reconciliation*)

Brownicity: The Art & Beauty of Living & Loving Beyond Race is the space we created to not only dream about the more beautiful world that our hearts know is possible but to **practice producing** that world. We are finding that practice achieves a lot more than just mastery. **Practice** also boosts confidence and bolsters proficiency. **Practice** allows us to tremendously grow our capacity as visionaries and creators—to boldly change the world.

ASK YOURSELF

Do I take the time to imagine the kind of society in which I'd love to live? What role would I play? How would I interact with others?

Am I creating the society for which I long? Or am I simply responding to the world that someone else created?

REACH

1. How will you continue to move forward with the process of being transformed and engaging in transformative action?

2. What do you need to do?

3. Will you practice new beliefs, thoughts, and actions?

4. How will you actively disconnect from the race narrative?

5. Will you engage in resources offering truth?

6. Will you forgive sources of false beliefs (e.g. church, parents, community, school, country)?

REACH BEYOND WHERE YOU ARE NOW

1. Set action goals for yourself, your family, and communities where you have influence.

2. Acknowledge your fears and purpose to move past them.

3. Enlist accountability friends.

MEDITATION AND PRAYER

May we be people of peace,
With voices of hope,
Doing the hard work of love.

⑩
CONCLUSION

Race is powerful nonsense!
— *(Dismantling Racism Workshop,*
Race Matters for Juvenile Justice, Charlotte, NC)

Have you completed all the chapter assignments? Are the blank spaces that were reserved for note-taking and reflective journaling now overflowing with your notes, personal reflections, and answers? Do you understand why the 'four false starts,' mentioned in the first chapter, do not offer enough substance for healthy race conversations? Do you have more questions?

The impact of race/ism on our lives is undeniable. In chapters one and two, we acknowledged the flaws of popular race/ism discourse, and set the tone and pace for a journey of renewing our minds. In order to move forward, we must indeed move forward differently. This journey, grounded in Romans 12:2, is not about affirming an 'I'm not racist' status. Instead, we gained a solid beginning to what will be a life-long journey of dismantling race/ism, a man-made construct that fundamentally opposes what God finds good, pleasing and complete.

Race/ism is like gravity, in that most of us know about it, but can not explain how it actually works. Most people don't know the laws or physics that make gravity happen. Likewise, we see and talk about the evidence and outcomes of race/ism—e.g. segregated churches, communities, and schools, opportunity gaps, and the prison industrial complex—but lack an understanding of how it all manifested—the ideology, the "science," the economic incentives, the social engineering, and the belief systems and laws that created it and hold it in place.

So, in chapters three, four and five, we learned what most of us do not know about race/ism, but need to understand in order to create change.

While the early chapters provided an educational foundation, chapters six, seven and eight, continued to build on that foundation by expanding our analysis of race/ism. We examined how representations and stereotypes have shaped and informed our consciousness and decision making. We took a critical look at how policies created to serve some, have actually disadvantaged others.

And finally, chapter nine encourages us to put feet to our prayers—to actively and intentionally create change.

What LIES Between Us offers this paradox: Race/ism was created by our country's founders. It us unfortunate that at a point in our nation's history, leaders deemed race/ism necessary for the success of our country. However, to know that race/ism was created by men driven by self-interests, means that like any man-made kingdom, it can fall. We can dismantle race/ism and create a more beautiful world.

We don't have to be defeated and determined by the lie, ideology, and legacy of race. We have been endowed by the Creator with a creative power to overthrow this destroyer of souls and lives.

We can renew our minds. We can switch on our brains, question everything, no longer passively accept information that dehumanizes people, and embrace the responsibility to reject the LIES we've inherited.

We can choose a frame of justice, love, grace, mercy, friendship, forgiveness, and ONEness. And within that frame, we can write narratives that speak to the God-value in all of us. We actually can live, move, and "be" very differently than we are now. But we have to intentionally reach for it!

Dr. Lucretia Carter Berry

Dr. Lucretia Carter Berry is co-founder of Brownicity: The Art & Beauty of Living & Loving Beyond Race. Her expression through Brownicity is an intersection of her passion for ONEness work, her faith, her love for family, and her professional experience as an educator.

As a college professor, Dr. Berry designed curriculum and taught in teacher education programs on issues of race, diversity and educational technology. Currently, she is a wife to Nathan and a mom of three magical girls—Sinclair, London and Quinn.

BROWNICITY

Brownicity / broun' isədē /
pronounced like "'ethnicity"
noun.

A combination of the words "brown" and "ethnicity." Brown represents melanin, the pigment we all have. Ethnicity means "that which we have in common." Essentially, we are all hues of brown. We are many hues but one humanity.

Brownicity: The Art & Beauty of Living & Loving Beyond Race is our platform for disrupting the race narrative and its legacy of racism. We are family-focused and dedicated to advocacy, education and support for racial healing and anti-racism.

Brownicity is encouraging, inspiring, helpful, and hopeful while promoting ONEness, healing, and change. WE are proof that love defies race/ism! And we want to spread the LOVE!